*A Daddy's Girl*

**Other books by Trisha L. King:**

*Love 2.0: Poetry for the Soul*

# A Daddy's Girl

### Trisha L. King

WestBow
PRESS®
A DIVISION OF THOMAS NELSON
& ZONDERVAN

Copyright © 2017 Trisha L. King.

All rights reserved. No part of this book may be used or reproduced by any means, graphic, electronic, or mechanical, including photocopying, recording, taping or by any information storage retrieval system without the written permission of the author except in the case of brief quotations embodied in critical articles and reviews.

WestBow Press books may be ordered through booksellers or by contacting:

WestBow Press
A Division of Thomas Nelson & Zondervan
1663 Liberty Drive
Bloomington, IN 47403
www.westbowpress.com
1 (866) 928-1240

Because of the dynamic nature of the Internet, any web addresses or links contained in this book may have changed since publication and may no longer be valid. The views expressed in this work are solely those of the author and do not necessarily reflect the views of the publisher, and the publisher hereby disclaims any responsibility for them.

Any people depicted in stock imagery provided by Thinkstock are models, and such images are being used for illustrative purposes only.
Certain stock imagery © Thinkstock.

ISBN: 978-1-5127-8890-7 (sc)
ISBN: 978-1-5127-8891-4 (hc)
ISBN: 978-1-5127-8889-1 (e)

Library of Congress Control Number: 2017908263

Print information available on the last page.

WestBow Press rev. date: 06/22/2017

# Contents

Dedication ..................................................................... ix

## Part 1  Somewhere in Time

| | | |
|---|---|---|
| Chapter 1 | Daddy Speaks ............................................... 1 |
| | Number Four, Letter M .................................. 3 |
| | Four Here—To Go .......................................... 5 |
| | Again and Again ............................................. 7 |
| Chapter 2 | Mommy Speaks ............................................. 9 |
| | The Sound .................................................... 11 |
| | Ride ............................................................... 13 |
| Chapter 3 | Brand-New Life ............................................ 15 |
| | Baby Girl ....................................................... 17 |
| | Too Late? ...................................................... 19 |
| Chapter 4 | All Those Years Ago ..................................... 21 |
| | Daddy: "They Left" ...................................... 23 |
| | Grandma: "She Needs Us" ........................... 25 |
| | Mommy: "Thanks, Uncle" ........................... 27 |
| | Uncle: "All Aboard" ..................................... 29 |
| | Mommy: "Your Help" .................................. 31 |
| Chapter 5 | Letting Go .................................................... 33 |
| | Everything Changed .................................... 35 |
| | That Is Why ................................................. 37 |
| | Somewhere in Time ..................................... 39 |

## Part 2  Going Forward

| | | |
|---|---|---|
| Chapter 6 | Growing Up | 43 |
| | A New House | 45 |
| | Head Start | 47 |
| | My Beautiful Teachers | 49 |
| Chapter 7 | Special Girl? | 51 |
| | Gifted and Talented, but Not at Home | 53 |
| | Wordy | 55 |
| Chapter 8 | Yes, He Is | 57 |
| | Daddy's Little Girl? | 59 |
| | He's Not Your Dad | 61 |
| | First Name | 63 |
| Chapter 9 | Blended | 65 |
| | He's My Dad Now | 67 |
| | Adjustments | 69 |
| | Troubled | 71 |
| | Same Thing | 73 |
| Chapter 10 | Finding My Father's Love | 75 |
| | Daddy, God | 77 |

| | |
|---|---|
| Epilogue | 79 |
| What Is? | 81 |

| | |
|---|---|
| Acknowledgements | 83 |
| About the Author | 85 |

# Dedication

This book is lovingly dedicated to:
*My mom, Helen*

# Part 1

# Somewhere in Time

## Chapter 1

# Daddy Speaks

# Number Four, Letter M

Four is a number that I simply don't like,
And that should have been my warning
That something here just wasn't right.

Baby number four has arrived,
Man, oh, man.

So, the first thing I did was reach for baby's hand
To see the sign that she is mine.

But, it's not here.
In her hand, there are just random lines
That are barely there.

They don't form the letter *M*,
Those lines,
Like they do
For all babies of mine.

It just isn't there,
And how could this be?

In their hands, all my babies
Take after me.

I looked down at my hand on a whim,
And there it was, the letter *M*.

But not so with this baby,
baby number four.

*You* may think it's not right,
But now I'm mad to the core,
Cause this identifying mark
Is what *I* look for!

If she were mine, it would have been there
When she was born,
And for nine months
Thought she was mine—
I could've sworn.

But, this is an unexpected issue
That I refuse to skip.
So her mother and me,
This we'll have to deal with!

# Four Here—To Go

Cute baby, brown baby,
Welcome into this world, baby?

No, not really,
I don't welcome you at all, baby,
Cause I don't know
Whose baby you are,
Not mine, for sure.

And I told your mother that, and she played Miss Demure,
Pretending that it's not clear
That this baby here
Is not mine.

"How could you say that?"
I remember that was what she had said
As worry lines quickly filled her forehead.

She looked almost sincere with her beautiful face,
With her guard up just in case,
And she was right to judge so astutely,
Cause I knew how to twist and turn things just to suit me.

And similar to situations in the past,
Control of my anger, especially this time,
I could not grasp.
The more she feared, the worse it got.
The more she talked, the more unwilling I was to stop
Accusing her,
Cause I knew better than that.
She must have cheated on me behind my back.

My anger with this whole thing was very real,
And not for one moment more could I possibly deal.

"That baby is not mine!"
This I said as I threw the bottle of wine
That was to calm me,
Or so I was hoping,
Along with the dope that I had been smoking.

As it registered in my ears, the crash against the wall,
The woman who was my wife suddenly looked fragile and small,
Which enraged me the more,
So I backhanded her
And felt very glad as
She hit the
Floor.

Now, why did she go
And make
Me do that?

## Again and Again

Once was not enough,
It never was,
But this time I had to
Do it again, and again,
And again,
To let her know that,
In no uncertain terms,
Were her lies going to win.

This lesson, I decided,
She needed to learn,
As my left and right fists
Alternately, took turns
On her arms, on her legs, and on her face
As she held her body tight,
Trying to brace
Against the blows.

I did not want to stop
But I got tired,
I got winded,
And my mind
Felt crazy,
Like suspended
Somewhere in time.

So I stopped the assault
Against which she had not fought
Back,
Not even a little.

I walked away,
Heading toward the door,
Thought I heard her say something
Like she was looking for more.

But I was tired,
Tired to the bone,
Didn't even care that
I saw her reaching for the phone,
Didn't care
That she looked a mess

Maybe
About this here baby
She's ready now to confess.

CHAPTER 2

# Mommy Speaks

# The Sound

I tried to find the words
To say
My world
Had just ended
And
That I was alone and suspended
Somewhere in time.

But
The sound that came from my lips
Was heavy and thick,
And it sounded foreign to my own ears.
I could not get a grip
On my words,
And it was weird—
I couldn't get a word out
Is how it appeared.

My groans just filled the sound waves on the phone
As the voice asked if I was here alone.

Even to this,
I could not give an answer that was clear,
So
The voice on the line simply said,
"Help is near."
This voice was reassuring on the other end of the line.
It said, "Help is coming.
It's just a matter of time."

It asked questions,
But the answers I could not say.

So after a while
It got the message
And just repeated,
"Help's on the way."

The voice was pleasant
But somehow commanded my attention,
And as each minute went by,
"Help is on the way," is what it would mention.

But I think
The sound of the voice,
Lulled me to sleep,
Cause I could barely keep
Myself
Awake.

# Ride

The sirens sounded angry
as they got closer to the house.
And when help got here
The search was on for my spouse.

But he was gone, completely out of sight.
Otherwise he would have been locked up
That night.

They placed me on the gurney,
And it was that point
There
That began my journey
Without him.

Alone in the ambulance
Beside the attendant,
I had time to think
For more than a minute.

I was thankful that the other children had not been at home.
They saw none of that; to them, this time, it is unknown.
But the attendant said the baby would be brought to me soon,
Once I'd been securely placed in a hospital room.

I could not bear to leave her side,
But she could not come with me
On this ambulance ride.

The ride seemed extra long since my baby wasn't with me,
So I just laid there and offered up a litany
Of prayers.

They said they would let me feed her
After I was checked out.
They'd bring her to my room, so my milk she wouldn't be without.

But, understand, the temporary separation still broke my heart.
This
Was no way
For our baby to start
Life.

# Chapter 3
# Brand-New Life

# Baby Girl

You'd never know I'd had a rough start.
I was now three-and-a-half,
And my, did I know how to make my mommy laugh.

Smart and rather bright,
Had the ability to learn things
On first sight.

Loved to learn immensely,
Sharp, and thoughtful,
And loved life intensely.

This was me before my school days.
I was taking life in
In so many new ways.

I was home with Grandma every day,
And above everything else I loved to play.
Life was good and uncomplicated.
In fact, every day I just waited
For my siblings to get out of school.

A cute baby girl,
Chubby with dark-brown skin,
Big, brown eyes, an oval face,
And a soft, rounded chin.
Most days
My short hair was braided,
The top one parted
And pulled to the side,
And to be honest,
I have tried
To hide
The pride
Associated with
The pics
From that time!

# Too Late?

One day I had become aware
That there was a man sitting downstairs.
I had never seen him before and probably wasn't going to see him again,
But that was my dad, Grandma would explain later, every now and then.

She'd say he was trying to set things right, my dad was.
She'd say he wanted Mommy back in his life, cause
He missed her.

But Grandma would say she didn't know why he didn't come to the house more
To try to fight for his family, since he swore
He loved us.

She'd say that Mommy
Was doing well on her own.
She had a good job, a car, and helped Grandma out with her home.

She'd say he didn't try to help Mommy out
And that she was doing it all without
His help.

Grandma would say Mommy didn't need him anymore
And that the latch had completely closed on that once-open door.
She'd say
For him
It was too late.

## Chapter 4

# All Those Years Ago

# Daddy: "They Left"

I came home to see
That there was nobody home
Besides me.

No one was there—
No children, no wife.
Oh, God. This must be the end of my life.

How could I be so careless, to leave them alone?
Never thought for one moment she'd leave our home.

I wanted her back
And desperately—I realized that.
But it occurred to me that I needed a plan,
As I rolled the cigarette that was in my hand.
This will help me to think.

I sat back in my chair with much expectation
As the smoke cleared away my present devastation.

I'll go find her,
But first this is what I'll need
So I closed my eyes
And inhaled to breathe
In
Just a little.

# Grandma: "She Needs Us"

Brother, I need you to go get my daughter.
She's in need of your help,
And as her mom I still feel the pain
That night that she felt.

I cried the same bitter tears,
So go get my daughter before the worst of my fears
Come true.

Go get her and her four babies as soon as you can.
Please, go get her, now,
Away from that man.

I can't get her myself since I'm so far away,
So please do this for me.
Go get her today.

Don't alarm her husband.
You see, he must not know.
Just get her to me, with my grands in tow.

My grandson is six, my granddaughters are two,
And the newborn
Arrived the very day she was due.

Gather them, brother. Put them on a train.
Your effort this time cannot be in vain.
Her life depends on it—I believe this to be true.
So brother, please,
Go get my daughter and her four babies, too.

# Mommy: "Thanks, Uncle"

Uncle saw it in the newspaper,
The ruckus that was my life.

He saw the high cost I paid for being my husband's wife.
And for Uncle it wasn't the very first time
That he'd had to come by this house of mine.

But this time it was different, very different somehow.
Uncle said very sternly, "You're leaving with me now.
Your mother is crying to me on the phone,
So I'm gonna put you on a train bound for your new home."

He grabbed a suitcase and threw stuff in,
As I just stood there sorrowful for my husband's sin.

I knew this time Uncle was not going to leave without me,
So when he opened the door
I allowed myself
*This* time
To be free.

# Uncle: "All Aboard"

"You have to take care of your mom and three sisters,"
I had told her oldest, her son.
I had a little talk with him,
And he seemed very serious when we were done.

I said, "Little man,
Just last month I could count your age on one hand,
But now
Your mom is going to need you as you all travel alone.
She's going to need your help even after you get to your new home."

Yes,
He will have to rise to the occasion.
I told him this, and he solemnly agreed without further persuasion.

So I put them on the train
Bound for the northern states,
And only briefly I thought, *Could this be a mistake?*

But I allowed that thought in my mind to wane
As I settled the five of them safely on that northbound train.

# Mommy: "Your Help"

Lord, I need Your help.
I'm asking this and nothing more,
That since I'm now mommy *and* daddy to my four
That You help me to be a good parent on my own.

Help me to raise them well until they're grown.
Give me the strength that I will need
And wisdom and courage, Lord, I plead.

## Chapter 5
# Letting Go

## Everything Changed

Mom and Dad did separate right after my birth,
And I'm okay with that
For whatever it's worth.

Pain marked the beginning of my life.
Dad was no longer husband,
Mom, no longer wife.

Their marriage was troubled,
Truth be told,
But with the turmoil of my arrival,
Their bond
Was
Simply
Too weak to hold
Together.

# That Is Why

For a long time I did not know the truth behind their separation.
Daddy was just absent without explanation.

I didn't learn why he was not with us until I met him as an adult.

At age eighteen,
I met the man whom I had only once ever seen.

My dad cried. He wept.
He said it was from all those years that he was kept
From us.

I questioned that and learned that it wasn't quite true.
He only came back for us
One time, maybe two.

As I talked with family
And as I talked with him,
Echoes of a distant past
That had been so quiet
Now resonated in vast
Detail.

Dad had left us alone,
He thought, for the better,
And Mom,
Well, she was left with no choice but to sever
The ties
That she once had to him.

# Somewhere in Time

When I met Dad as an adult, he played me a song.
It was called
"Somewhere in Time."

And he told me how he wanted to make everything for me
Perfectly fine.

He looked at my hand and said,
"You have the letter *M*,"
And told me how that was so very important to him.

He said,
"It shows that you are mine, at long last,
And now if only I could erase the past."

He said,
"All my children have the letter *M* in their hands.
It's a dominant trait that I happen to pass on.
Each kid of mine was supposed to have this when they were born.

All those years ago, I thought your mother must have cheated,
And our discussion about your birth,
Well, it became rather heated!"

I looked down at my hand
And felt sorry for the man
Who was my dad.

He had missed out on our lives
Because of lies
He had told himself.

# PART II

# Going Forward

## Chapter 6
# Growing Up

# A New House

Mommy and Grandma had found a new house,
A big, white house there in the ghetto,
But with the move we soon realized that we had to let go
Of our old neighborhood friends.

This house was in a different part of the 'hood,
So with that we all quickly understood
That things had changed.

We still saw most of our friends at school during the week,
But we could no longer play with them outside on the street.

No, we had to make new friends for that.
But the kids on this block were less friendly,

Seemed a lot tougher, as a matter of fact.
They were not as nice as the kids we knew.
But after a while, we did make friends with a few.

And the house?
Well, it was just what the family seemed to need.
It was an old, three-story house, rather large, indeed.

The second and third floors were a full-functioning house.
That's where we lived,
And Grandma, on the first floor,
Was close by
To give
Mom a hand
When needed.

# Head Start

At four-and-a-half
I began Head Start,
A program that was a part
Of early child development for poor kids
In the ghetto
So we'd have an equal chance
With our fellow
Counterparts
Who lived in the suburbs.

So I went to Head Start every morning
And got picked up by Grandma around noon.

Grandma helped Mommy out a lot
And had even made room
In her other house
For us
Four-and-a-half years ago
When my mom and dad
Had called it quits,
Cause he used to hit
My mom.

But I didn't know anything
About that at all.

I was just concerned with
Having fun
And my finger paintings
Hanging on the wall
At Head Start.

## My Beautiful Teachers

My first teachers all had physical traits similar to mine:
Dark hair, dark skin, dark eyes,
Nothing loved, but nothing despised.

To me, just regular.
Nothing spectacular,
Just status quo.

But when I got to the very next grade,
Little did I know
That someone beautiful would be my teacher.
Someone who, to me, had striking features.

She had long hair, light eyes, and straight teeth.
She looked like all of the beautiful people I had seen on TV.

Never had I thought before I could possibly love a teacher more.
I didn't know much about this teacher,
But with just one glance,
I thought she looked extraordinarily nice,
And I didn't know why I thought these things,
Didn't even think twice.

But since I saw her, my favorite teacher was no longer the one.
This beautiful teacher took her title long before day number one
was even done.

But now I know I had been conditioned about what beauty is and was
And what this society deems as most loved,
Cause with physical traits like mine,
There was nothing and no one telling me I'm beautiful at any given time.

But now I see
In that role should've been my father,
My absent daddy.

But,
My beautiful teachers were there,
My aunties, cousins, teachers at the school, women at the church.
They all played a part in showing me what I'm worth.

In their own ways, they taught me to hold my head up and know,
That I'm good
Despite our very real struggle.

They taught me that,
I'm fearfully and wonderfully made,
And that forgiveness, humility, and love displayed
Are the true elements of beauty.

And yes, I now realize they also taught me
That my big, brown eyes, dark skin, and tightly curled hair,
Well,
They indeed made me a cutie!

# Chapter 7
# Special Girl?

# Gifted and Talented, but Not at Home

Early on, I was placed in the G&T class
Because I had
Excelled in school so far.
But at home I was still just the baby of four.

I was comfortable with that,
Wasn't looking for more,
But after a while it wasn't so easy being the baby
Because lately
Whenever there was a fight or dispute
My two sisters and brother seemed to forget
That I was their cute,
Baby sis.

I was getting older, so I had to adjust
And learn how not to make a fuss
over their new view of me.

I simply was growing up,
So I had to toughen up
And learn how to hold my very own,
There
In the crowded home.

Lately to them
I wasn't baby,
Nor was I even gifted or talented.

I was simply just
One kid in four.

So now
Somehow
I knew I wanted
More.

# Wordy

As I progressed in school,
I mastered grades one through three.
It seemed like Head Start must have worked for me.

My teachers were impressed with my ability to write.
Really, with words and me,
It was love at first sight.

My penmanship and stories were touted as the best,
But all that didn't matter to me, I guess.

I just loved to read and write,
And every chance I got, I read a new book,
And every day I couldn't wait to take a fresh look
Inside.

I held the words close,
And every day after school
I got another dose
Of
Words.

This was the perfect escape
That helped develop a skill.
I learned how to appeal
And how to make myself feel
A positive way
Just by writing
Words.

## Chapter 8
# Yes, He Is

# Daddy's Little Girl?

My mother had a friend, a companion,
A steady date.
He was over much of the time
And often stayed late.

Seemed like he was there all the time,
So in my young mind
He was daddy,
And I was his kid.

I didn't notice that no one else
Called him daddy like I did.
To me, I was his little girl,
And his presence always
Made my world
A better place to be.

I saw how Mommy smiled
And looked good
And how she always would
Be happy
When he was around.

And toward me he was protective, just like a dad,
Even scolded me when I was bad.

My mom met him
Long before I was even two,
So really him being there was all I ever knew.

So to me he was
Daddy.

# He's Not Your Dad

My siblings told me not to call him dad.
After all, he isn't our dad.

Our dad is nowhere to be found,
And although this man is always around,
He is not our dad!
I was told
At the rather ripe age of six years old,
No longer a baby
So maybe
I would understand.

So calling him dad, well that needed to stop,
But they never once considered how this change would rock
My world.

# First Name

I went back and forth between calling him daddy
And calling him nothing at all.

After my siblings had the talk with me,
In his presence I didn't know how to be.

He is not my dad?
This information really hurt my heart.
But I supposed that I'd better start
Addressing him differently.

I now noticed that my siblings called him by his first name
And that they expected of me to do
The same.

So I called him nothing
Cause I could not bring myself to do it,
And I'm very sure that he knew it.

He went from daddy to nothing at all
Simply because
I was no longer too small
To know the truth.

## Chapter 9

# Blended

# He's My Dad Now

He and Mommy were getting married.
I heard her tell someone that on the phone
One day when I was home
From school.

We will be moving in!
With his two kids and him.
He had a cute single home on the outskirts of town, a pool,
Two dogs, one white, one brown.

This was like a dream to me.
I could now call him dad legitimately
Without hearing my siblings fuss,
Cause now he's going to be dad
To all of us!

It was exciting, but the house was kinda small to take on four kids.
It didn't meet our needs like Grandma's house did.

Space was at a premium,
And we three girls had to share a rather *small*—medium—
Bedroom.

And my brother had no room to call his own,
Mostly cause our stepbrothers were both too grown
To share their room with him.

This arrangement was rough,
But back then
I didn't really take note.
I was just happy that now I could gloat
About calling him daddy once again.

## Adjustments

Going to my new school where very few kids looked like me
Was my first real encounter of being considered a minority.

I was asked questions about my hair and skin,
Felt like I lived in a time realm from way back when.

"How do you know when you're dirty and need a bath?"
Was one question that one kid dared to ask.
He thought my skin was too dark to see
And wondered if I bathed, like him, regularly.

Despite my experiences,
I was happy to be at my new school,
And I worked really hard as a general rule.

And I met new friends who liked me for me
And didn't look at race or treat me differently.

Everything in life seemed to be going just fine,
Until the end of our blended story
Was not far behind.

# Troubled

Mommy and Daddy were at odds a lot.
She often seemed hurt, as though she never forgot
Her painful history,
And for sure
It seemed that
They each felt differently
About our blended family situation.

He felt
Everything was good.
She felt
That he just never would
Make any real room in his heart
For us kids
Like she did with his.

She said he never talked to us
Even though we were all under the same roof,
And the fact that he couldn't name any conversation
To her
Was proof
That she was right.

# Same Thing

Ultimately, though,
We did end up moving back to the ghetto.

Our blended family had come to an end.
My siblings were teens. I was age ten.

Still, on all of us this had an impact.
In fact,
As we entered this familiar place in time,
It was hard
To leave even a difficult unity,
To return to an unsafe and impoverished community.

Really,
I just couldn't understand why their marriage didn't make it.
Deep inside I wondered if he just couldn't take it—
The noise,
Or the house that struggled to stay neat,
Or the fights we kids had where we would physically compete
Against one another.

Maybe it was a mixture of it all,
But that didn't take the pain away
That I had in my heart each and every day
From losing
A daddy's love in my life
Once again.

## Chapter 10
# Finding My Father's Love

# Daddy, God

Just call Him Daddy.
He's your Abba, Father,
The minister had said.

And as he spoke,
This novel idea truly filled my heart and head.

I had felt insignificant prior to this,
But what I just heard
My heart didn't miss.

You mean the Creator of all
Considers and calls
Me
His child?

You mean there is a love so deep
And that as His child I will reap
Benefits unrestrained
And that there's a heritage exclusively named
For me?

I can call Him Father, Daddy, Dad,
Whatever my heart desires to be so.

Finally I felt
I'd found acceptance
And an unconditional daddy's love
That will never let go!

# Epilogue

# What Is?

What is the Father's love in us?

Well,
It's understanding.
It's the feeling—despite the odds—on which we are standing.

It's warmth and complete honesty.
It's the undertaking of not taking ourselves too seriously.

It's the knowing that on God we can always depend.
It's a love letter already postmarked, sealed, and ready to send.

It's the setting up of the next generation to rise higher than the one before.
It's an unneeded doorbell on a perpetually open door.

It's a perfect, yet not-so-perfect, delivery and execution.
It's the communication of positive feelings sans dilution.

It's the hitting of the mark on exactly what's needed.
It's the taking of a stand when you can easily be seated.

It's the magic in a child's pretend magic potion.
It's the heartstrings that allow pulling and the heart that remains open.

It's the declaration of a blood-washed people that says, "Yes, we can win!"
It's the brave soul who presses stop, reset, and begin.

It's the future, present, and also what was.
It's all the good that you can ever think of.

It's the heart in the struggle with eyes set above.

These are the many,
Many ways
That we express
Our Father's
Love.

Poem from *Love 2.0: Poetry for the Soul*

# Acknowledgements

I am very grateful to my husband, Edwin King and our daughter, Victoria for their continual support of my writing. Thank you guys for being my everything.

Many, many thanks to my sisters, Rachele and Meredith who critiqued and helped develop early versions of the manuscript. Thank you for your pointers, suggestions and very real emotions that helped sway the direction of the story.

Special thanks to Jacki Heads for my author photos. Thank you for the sacrifice of your time and talent. The photography is absolutely wonderful.

My deepest gratitude to my mother, Helen for consistently encouraging me to write, even from a very early age. Thank you, Mom. I hope this work makes you proud.

# About the Author

Trisha L. King has a passion for writing and inspiring readers through poetry. Through a beautiful, poetic rhythm, she loves to tell the story of how God's love unfolds in areas where we don't always look – even in the routine and sometimes troubling aspects of life.

The poetry in her two publications, *Love 2.0: Poetry for the Soul* and *A Daddy's Girl*, is inspirational, thought-provoking and uplifting and motivates the reader to learn more about God's unconditional love.

**Enjoy this excerpt from Trisha L. King's e-book *Love 2.0: Poetry for the Soul***

# Love 2.0:
## Poetry for the Soul

TRISHA KING

# Ok ... Now Look Up

The pain is real.
Our back is against the wall
And just when we think we rise,

We climb,
But fall.

To the right, we look
But to no avail,
To the left, we look
Still we don't prevail,

Behind, we look
And we see our pain.
Forward, we look,
And we view the same.

But what about our successes?
O yes, our success!

Our success is shrouded
With dark, gray cloud,
Where lightening violently flashes,
And thunder claps loud.

Where rain pelts our face,
And water runs deep.
Where waves forever linger,
Rise and peak.

Strongholds,
Since times of old.

Some drink to this or that to disguise the sorrow,
And some smoke that stuff, to laugh

At the pain
That we face on tomorrow.

Our back is against the wall,
And just when we rise
we find, we fall.

To the left, right, behind and forward, we look,
But we have a Word from above.

Oh, sisters tell your brothers,
Brothers tell your sisters,
That now is the time.
Really, it is.

Now is the time
To look up.

## Kelven and His Friends

When Grandma comes home
After being with church folk
The house is always filled,
With the smell of liquor and cigarette smoke.

Girls always hanging around and on the phone,
Kelven doesn't seem to care that it's *her* home.

*Lord God, look on Kelven.*

He's only 15-years-old
But,
He's doing bad things now, I'm told.
Skipping school,
Drinking,
Smoking weed.
This Grandma sees, so
She tells him, "Son, it's Jesus you need."
He talks back to her,
As if she was the child, the teen,
Like *she* is the extra mouth *he* needs to feed.
Grandma looks away and says, "Satan, the Lord rebuke you."
But Kelven gets mad and begins to leave.
Because he doesn't have a clue,
exactly what she means.

*Lord, help me to be a light to Kelven.*
*God, somehow, someway*
*Help him hear me without him laughing,*
*About the things I need to say.*
*I need to tell him about Your love for him,*
*And how You long to be his friend, again.*
*How You're calling him by name,*

*How with me you did the same.*

*Lord God, look on Kelven.*

Now,
Kelven walks out and lets the screen door bang,
And goes down the street so that he can hang,
With his boys.

He quickly forgets
The argument,
Lights up the cigarette,
That he was hiding from her.
He feels okay now since he's huddled with the rest of the guys on the street corner.

To Kelven and his friends,
A good education, a job, and a respectable place in the community,
Is a figment of someone's
Imagination, and not a real opportunity.

Not making excuses, just stating how they feel,
They're smart, they see and realize
What mostly happens when they become men.
Dismissed, not given a chance,
And often ending up in somebody's prison.

*But God can you look on Kelven?*

*God, can you draw Kelven to you.*
*Let him know, that as Your son, Lord, him, you will defend.*
*Lord, if you save Kelven, it only takes one,*
*His life can be the catalyst that saves even his friend.*

*And the next friend, and the next one, and the next...*

## Nothing Beyond Me

I was small.
But I knew what I was looking at.
You tried to be discreet,
And tried to sell it only on the street

But my eyes saw what you did not want me to see
Those undercover exchanges
The *this* for *that*,
The stash always hidden behind your back

I saw it all.
You showed me a world that seemed so small—
Not much in it,
You taught me that money was the bottom line,
And that love isn't.

You felt there was nothing beyond you,
And beyond *your* own need, you could not see.
So ultimately I saw,
There's nothing beyond me.

You could not see beyond you,
Or how your secret exchanges hurt others beyond you.
How it hurt people, families, and the community,
And how it hurt your child, yes, how it hurt me.

Now I'm walking in your shoes,
And I too got little ones looking on.
But it doesn't bother me now,
They can do whatever they've got to do to get by.

And if it means selling that stuff to a fiend to get by,
I have no worries.
Cause you taught me
That there is nothing beyond that big, blue
Sky.

No God, no Lord watching over me and mine,
Yes.
You taught me just fine—
This thing that I see,
That there is absolutely nothing at all,
Beyond me.

# What If Jesus Returned Today?

What if Jesus returned today?
And that it's true, all that you had heard people say.

That He's the Way, the Truth, and the Life,
And now He's come back for the Church, His wife.

The Church, the billions of people—
That believe that what He said is simple.
Knowing that the truth is basic,
No matter how hard people try to make it.

Love God and love each other.

Those who grab a hold of this truth
And live their lives in this way,
Would be among the first ones who'd get to see Him today.

Those who don't get the love message,
Perhaps know the golden rule, and *this* do.
Treat others the way you want them to treat you.

That is a principal from which you can start.
Just add Jesus, the love activating part.

Once the love ingredient you genuinely get,
You'll see loving God and loving people is for
what you were meant.

Real love means loving others who may be different from you,
It means treating them the same, as those
to whom you relate to.

If everyone would understand this elementary message and
put it to practice everyday,
To any and everyone they'd meet or may affect along their way,
The world would change in leaps and bounds,
And the resulting impact would be — profound!

Deep down, we all know this to be true.
But to exhibit care and love — some people refuse to do.

They have their own interests that come first and do not want to bend.
Not caring about others — even though we're all human.

These folks may want to reconsider their stance on life
In a more meaningful way.

Cause it's always a possibility,
Even if you think remote — that Jesus *could* return today.

Printed in the United States
By Bookmasters